Excel for Children:
An enjoyable and intuitive introduction to basic spreadsheet

Excel for Children:
An enjoyable and intuitive introduction to basic spreadsheet

Ali Akbar & Zico Pratama Putra

Kanzul Ilmi Press

2019

First Printing: 2019

ISBN: 9781799212843

Editor: Zico Pratama Putra

Kanzul Ilmi Press
Woodside Ave.
London, UK

Bookstores and wholesalers: Please contact Kanzul Ilmi Press email

zico.pratama@gmail.com.

Trademark Acknowledgments

LEARNING EXCEL

Microsoft Excel is primary software in MS Office package. Microsoft. Excel is used to do spreadsheet analysis, and Access is used to do some relational database data operation. This two software can be used to help any of your office needs.

Pic 1 Excel and Access, two most important software in MS Office

1.INTRODUCTION TO EXCEL

Microsoft Excel is the most important and most famous spreadsheet app used in businesses and offices around the world. Excel can be used as a spreadsheet calculator for every type of business. This is a universal spreadsheet app that is easy to be learned.

An Excel app, has many features, such as calculations and graphics creations. Since this program is straightforward to be learned, Excel becomes the most popular spreadsheet app today.

MS Excel used on many platforms, such as windows, or Macintosh. Excel already released on Mac OS Since version 5.0 on 1993.

Right now, MS Excel is an integral part of the Microsoft Office package.

Pic 2 Office 2018 logo

1.1 Running Excel

Running Excel can be done using many techniques. If you use Win 8 or above, click Start > All Programs > Microsoft Office then click Excel. Or you may use **Run** window by clicking Windows + R then type and execute "Excel" command.

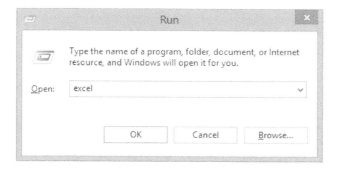

Pic 3 Typing "Excel" command to run MS Excel

A splash screen will shown:

Pic 4 Splash screen Excel 2018

1.2   Creating Workbook

The workbook is an Excel file. This can be used to save all the information you need. To be able to perform a spreadsheet calculation, you need to create a workbook first.

Here are steps you can do to create a workbook:

1. After Excel window shown, click on the Blank Workbook:

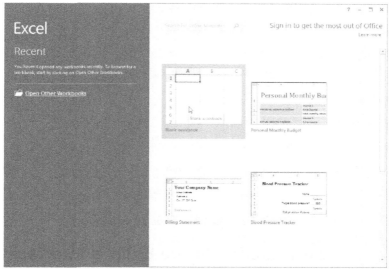

Pic 5 Click on the Blank Workbook to create a workbook

2. An empty workbook will be set up but hasn't yet saved. You will do spreadsheet calculation here.

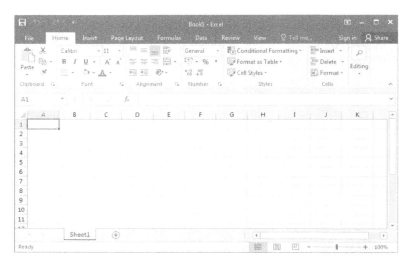

Pic 6 Excel 2018 workbook interface

1.3　Introduction to the Excel's Interfaces

To be able to work with Excel, you have to know first, the functions of buttons and other interfaces of Excel.

1.3.1 Quick Access Toolbar

Quick Access Toolbar is a toolbar on the top left of your Excel app. You can access commands quickly using this toolbar because you don't have to open ribbon tabs. On its initial condition, Quick Access Toolbar only have three buttons, Save, Undo, and Repeat.

Pic 7 Quick access toolbar

But you can also add other buttons or commands to make your access to those buttons faster. Here are steps you can do to add buttons to quick access toolbar:

1. Click on the arrow icon on the right side of quick access toolbar.

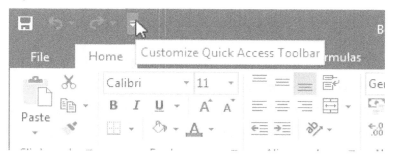

Pic 1.8 Menu to Customize Quick Access Toolbar

2. Choose the command button you want to add. To select other commands, click **More Commands**.

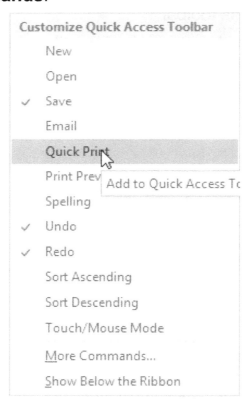

Pic 1.9 Menu to insert new button to quick access toolbar

3. If it's already entered and has a checked sign, the command button will add to quick access toolbar.

Pic 10 new button already added to Quick Access Toolbar

1.3.2 Name box

Name box will display the selected cell's name. If you choose a range (more than one cells), this will show range's identity. For example, if cell B4 is being selected, name box will display "B4", that shows the selected column is B and the selected row is 4.

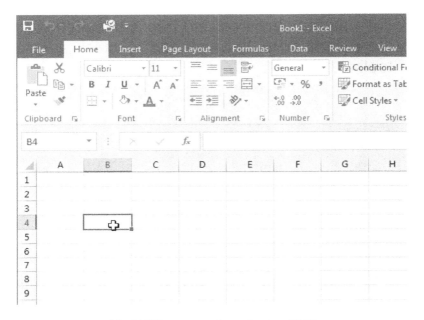

Pic 11 When name box display "B4".

1.3.3 Formula Bar

You can insert data, or edit data using formula bar. For example, when cell B2 entered "2018", you will find formula bar like this.

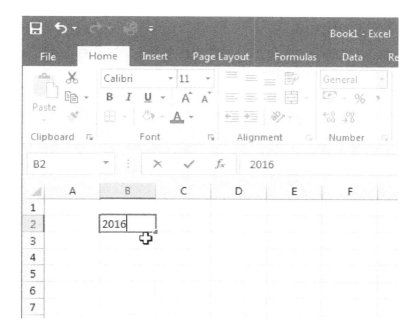

Pic 12 Formula bar when a user enters content to cell B2.

1.3.4 Ribbons

Ribbons contain all commands needed to perform calculations, formatting, etc. They have many ribbons dedicated to each function, such as Home, Insert, Page Layout, etc. Just click the tab of the ribbon, it'll display the buttons inside the ribbon.

Pic 13 Ribbon in Excel

1.3.5 Column

The column is the vertical part of the cell. In Excel, column identified by alphabets, such as A, B, C and so forth.

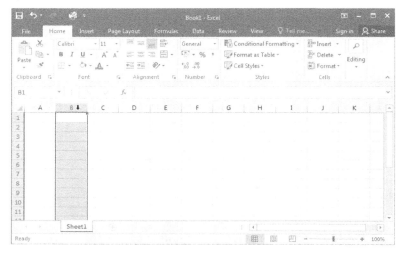

Pic 14 Column B selected

1.3.6 Row

The row is the horizontal part. You can choose a row on its left. In Excel, row identified by a number.

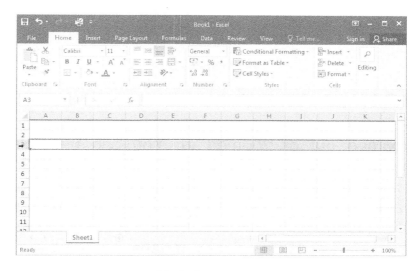

Pic 15 Row in Excel

1.3.7 Worksheet

If Excel file is a workbook, then a sheet in Excel spreadsheet is called worksheet. A workbook may have more than one worksheet. When a workbook created, there will be on worksheet created by default. In the older version of Excel, there were three sheets available.

You can rename, add, and delete worksheets.

1.3.8 Horizontal Scroll Bar

Horizontal scrollbar used to scroll worksheet's position on Excel. You can slide the scroll bar or click the right arrow or left arrow button.

Pic 16 Scrollbar

1.3.9 Zoom Control

The size of the spreadsheet display can be zoomed out or zoomed in. You can use this button to do so. Just click and drag zoom slider to make the image larger or smaller. The zoom value can be seen on the right. Standard is 100%. If more than 100% means greater, if less than   100%   means   lower.

Pic 17 Zoom control to control the zoom

1.4   Open Workbook

To open a workbook, you can perform steps below:

1. Click File tab.

2. Click Open. You will see the window below:

Pic 18 File > Open top menu to open Excel file

3. Choose the file you want to open:

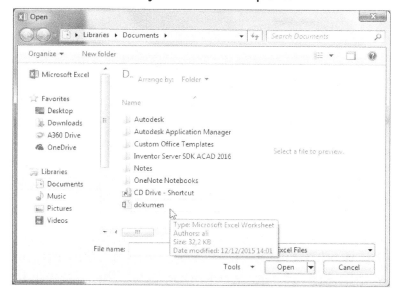

Pic 19 Select the file to open

4. You can also open in another place, like OneDrive or in the network.

5. Click the **Open** button, and the file will be opened.

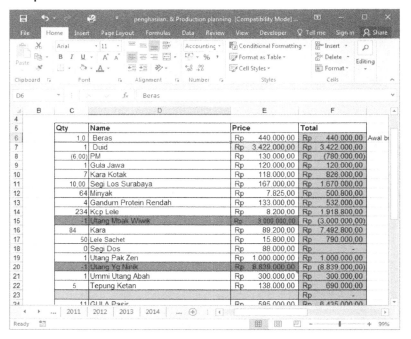

Pic 20 Workbook opened

1.5   Saving Workbook

If the workbook created already, you can change the content of the workbook and then save the workbook again. Saving means the change you created will be permanently implemented.

To save, you just click CTRL + S shortcut on the keyboard. Or click the Diskette button on quick access toolbar.

Pic 21 Diskette icon on quick access toolbar to save the workbook

You can also click from File ribbon. Click the File > Save. This will open Save As window if you haven't saved the file before. You can save it into OneDrive, local PC or another place in the network by clicking **Add a Place**.

Pic 22 Click Save to save into this PC

2. CELL OPERATIONS

A cell is an intersection between a row and a column. You can put a value on a cell. You can also create functions, and do some data calculation here.

2.1 Modify Column, Row, and Cell

A column has a uniform width, but you can enlarge or constrict column's width. To modify column width, you can do steps below:

1. Put your pointer between column. The pointer will change its icon like below:

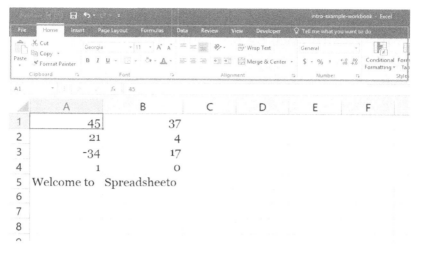

Pic 23 Put pointer below

2. Slide right to increase the column's width. The pixel size of the column's width will emerge, you can slide it to match the size you want.

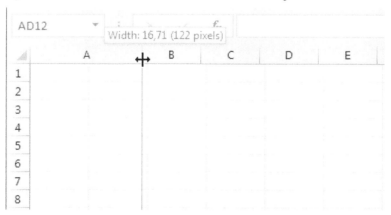

Pic24 Click and drag to change the column's width

3. If you release the drag click, the new width of the column will be implemented.

Pic 25 Column's width after changed

4. If you want to change the column's width precisely using the pixel's number size, then click the column's header, right-click and choose **Column Width** menu.

Pic 26 Choose Column Width menu

5. Enter the column's width in pixel. Click OK.

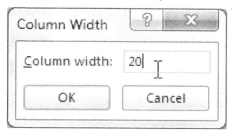

Pic 27 Entering the pixel value in Column Width

6. The column will change its width according to the pixel value inserted.

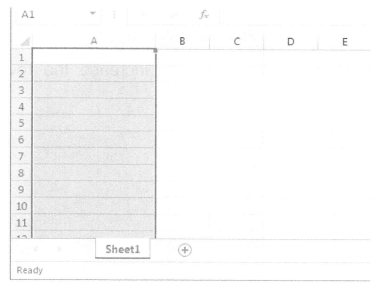

Pic 28 Column width after modified by adding the pixel value

For rows, the method is similar. You can do it using steps below:

1. Put the pointer on the border between rows. The pointer will change its icon like this pic below:

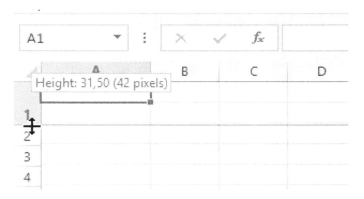

Pic 29 Pointer's icon changed

2. Click and drag below to increase the row's size.

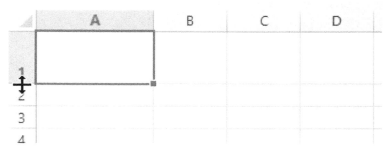

Pic 30 Sliding the pointer's icon to resize the row

3. If you want to enter the new pixel size of the row, just click row's header on the left, then click **Row height** menu.

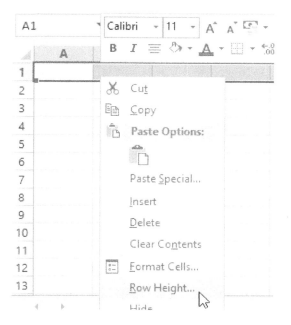

Pi c31 Right-click and choose Row height menu

4. Insert the new row height value in the pixel, and click **OK**.

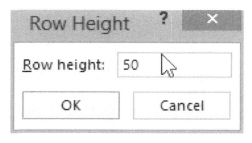

Pic 32 Inserting the new row height value in pixel

5. The row's size will be updated.

Pic 33 Row's height updated

2.2   Formatting Cell

The content of a cell can be formatted using these techniques:

1. For example, the cell B4 has a regular number like the pic below; we'll format it.

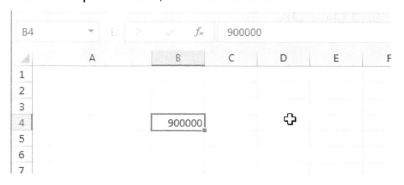

Pic 34 Cell B3 that will be formatted

2. Right-click on the cell, and choose **Format Cells** menu.

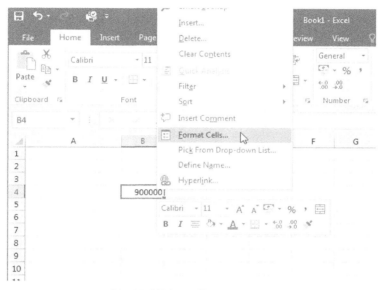

Pic 35 Click on Format Cells menu

3. Because the data type of the cell's content is a number, a Number tab will appear. On Number tab, you can choose the number's type, whether it will be a general number, currency, etc.

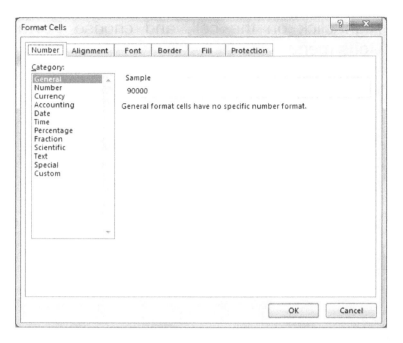

Pic 36 Number tab

4. To create a currency, click on Currency on Category box. Then choose a symbol for the currency, and choose the decimals amount needed.

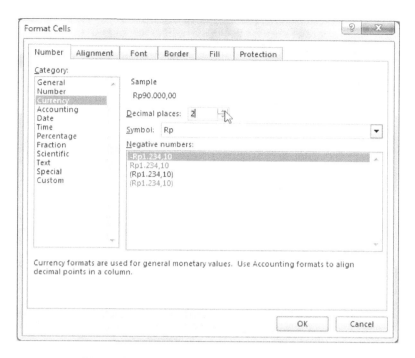

Pic 37 Configuring the currency's formatting

5. On the Alignment tab, you can set up the text's alignment on the cell. You can also change the degree of orientation of the text by changing the direction of the text on Orientation box, or by entering the degree value on numeric up down box **Degrees**.

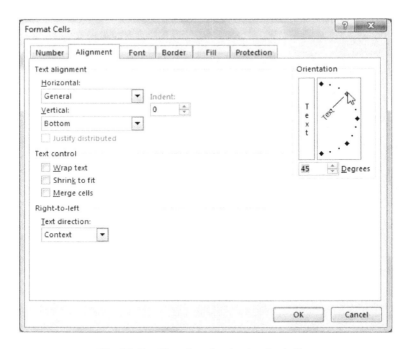

Pic 38 Configuring the text orientation

6. Click the Font tab to set up the font name, font style, and font size of the text on the cell.

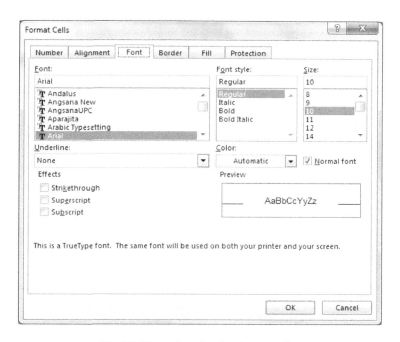

Pic 39 Changing the font properties

7. On the Border tab, you can create and define edge type and styles. You can choose line type of the edge and which part of the cells are bordered.

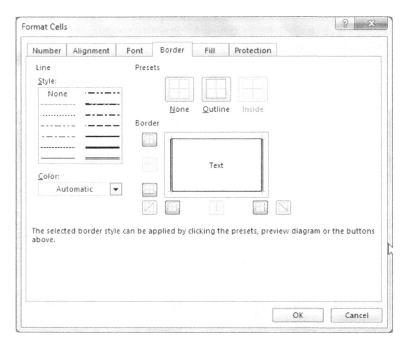

Pic 40 Changing border

8. On the **Fill** tab, you can modify the background color of the cell. Modify the value on Fill > Background color. You can also implement a pattern by selecting the Pattern Color and Pattern Style combo box.

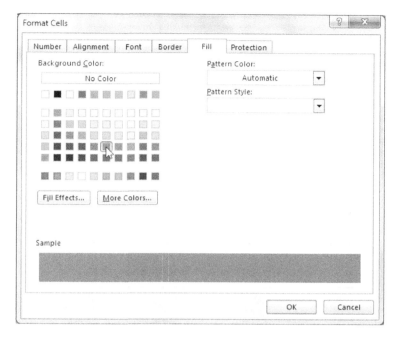

Pic 41 Changing Fill properties

9. Click **OK**, the cell and the text inside will be modified according to the selected format.

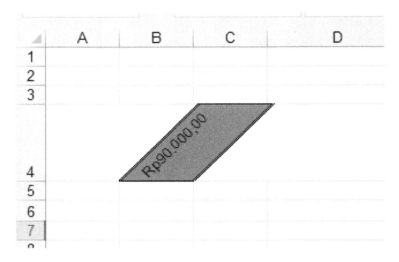

Pic 42 Cell and text already changed

3. WORKSHEET BASICS

A worksheet is a place where data calculation is performed. There are some basic spreadsheet operations you have to understand.

3.1   Add Worksheet

The new worksheet can be added using steps below:

1. Look at the plus sign below the Excel window, right on the worksheet's name. Click on that plus sign.

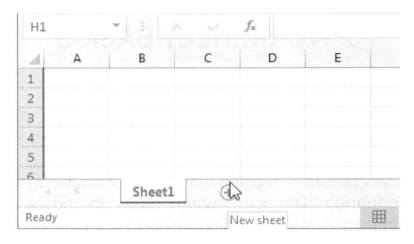

Pic 43 Click on plus button to add a new worksheet

2. A new sheet will emerge with the default name Sheet(Before+1).

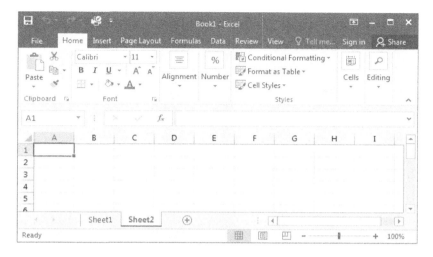

Pic 44 New sheet emerge

3. You can also use right-click method to create a new sheet, right-click on the sheet's tab and click **Insert**.

Pic 45 Clicking the Insert menu to add a new worksheet

4. An Insert window will emerge, choose the new type of sheet you want to add.

Pic 46 Select the new type of sheet

5. You can also create new sheet from existing templates just click the Spreadsheet solutions and click OK. Lots of templates available, such as sales report, billing statement, etc. You can see the preview in Preview box.

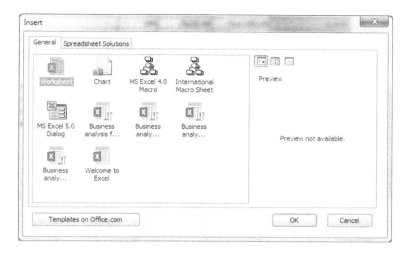

Pic 47 Insert template

6. If you create a new sheet from a template, the newly created sheet will have some data inside. You can edit or delete this data if you need it.

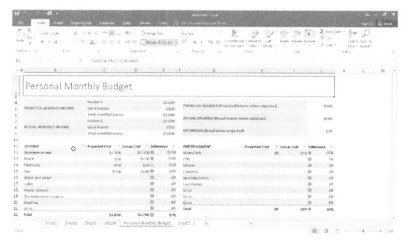

Pic 48 New sheet created with the template will have data inside it

37

3.2 Delete Worksheet

The worksheet can be deleted from the workbook. Here is how to delete existing worksheet:

1. Right-click on the sheet's tab you want to delete.

2. Click on **Delete** menu to delete it.

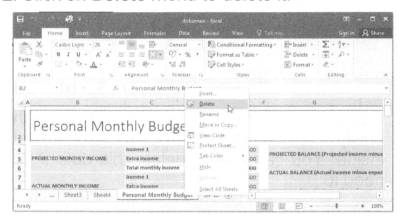

Pic 49 Click on Delete menu to delete a sheet

3. The sheet that is removed will be no longer accessible.

Pic 50 Sheets tab after deletion

3.3 Change the Sheets Order

Sheets inserted into the workbook will have order according to the time it's inserted. But you can change the sheet's order by drag and drop.

1. For example the initial condition like this, we want to change the Sheet1 position after Sheet2.

Pic 51 Initial sheets order

2. Click on Sheet1 then drag right after the Sheet2's position.

Pic 52 Drag Sheet1 to Sheet 2 position

3. Release the drag click, the sheet1's position will slide to the right of Sheet2's position.

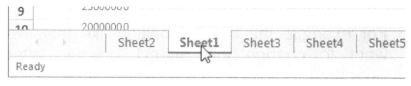

Pic 53 Sheet1's position

3.4   Rename Sheet

Sheet inserted will have default names like sheet2, sheet3, etc. You can change the sheet's name to make the sheet more readable.

1. To change the sheet's name, double-click on the sheets' name. The sheet's name will be selected like this:

Pic 54 Double-click on sheet's name

2. Type the new name.

Pic 55 Type the new name

3. Click Enter on your keyboard, the new name will be inserted

Pic 56 New name will be inserted

4. You can rename from right-click menu, just right click on the sheet's name and click **Rename** menu.

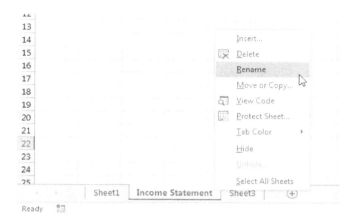

Pic 57 Click Rename menu

5. Type the new name. The new name will be implemented.

Pic 58 Type new name

3.5   Page Layout

Not only can be used as a tool to do spreadsheet calc, but Excel can also deliver the result to printed paper. Before you can print, you have to open the **Page Layout** tab on the ribbon that accommodates many features of page layout.

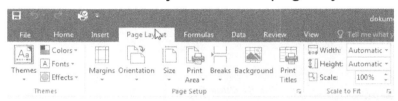

Pic 59 Page Layout tab

Click Themes and choose a theme you want for your whole spreadsheet. The theme you choose will automatically change the text, color, and font of your worksheet.

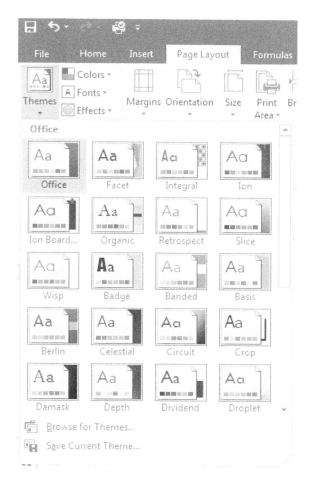

Pic 60 Theme list

Click Margins > Custom Margins to configure your margin. The margin is a whitespace between the end of the printed area to the end of the paper. If the margin you choose is not available on the list, you can create your Custom Margin.

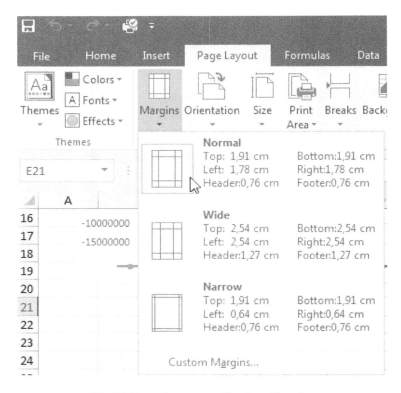

Pic 61 Menu to access Custom Margins

Then define the top, right, bottom and left margins. You can set margin for header or footer also.

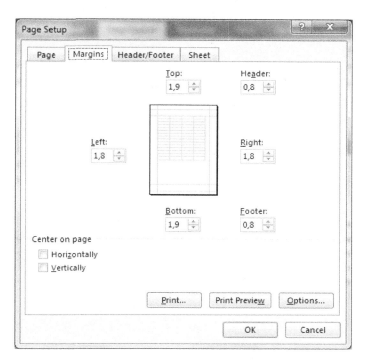

Pic 62 Defining custom margin

Paper orientation can be selected between portrait (vertical) or landscape (horizontal).

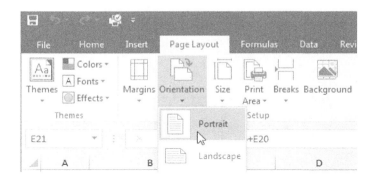

Pic 63 Changing paper orientation

To change paper size, click **Size** and choose the paper   type.

Pic 64 Selecting the paper size

Print Area section used to set printing area from the worksheet. Not all worksheet will be printed. You can set a certain part of the area to be printable.

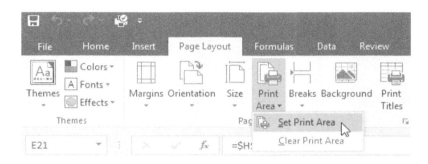

Pic 65 Set Print Area

Background used to insert background to the worksheet.

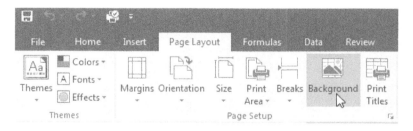

Pic 66 Click on the Background tab

You can choose image source, from the local file or Bing Image Search. Bing is owned by Microsoft, so MS Office support Bing rather than Google Image Search.

Pic 67 Locate image source for worksheet background

Just enter the keyword for your background image search, after that the result will be available in seconds.

Pic 68 Images available for the background image on Bing Image Search

If you have no internet connection, you can choose local images.

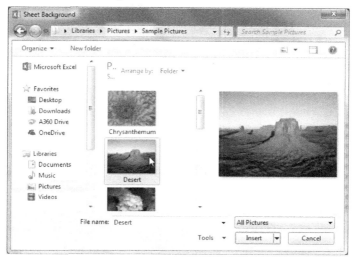

Pic 69 Locate image from the local computer

After the background image inserted the background are of your worksheet will be no plain anymore.

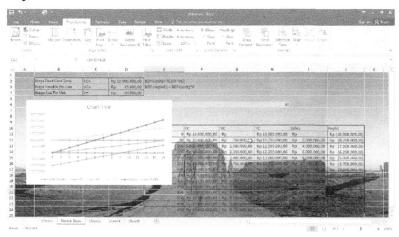

Pic 70 Worksheet condition after background image inserted

If you want to delete the background, just click the **Page Layout > Delete Background**.

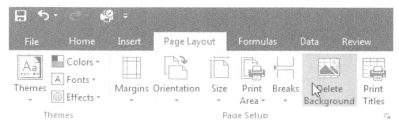

Pic 71 Clicking Delete Background button to delete the background

If you want to customize the Page Setup, click the arrow on the right bottom side of the Page Setup box in Page Layout ribbon.

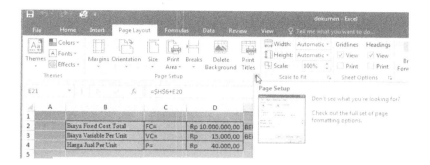

Pic 72 Button to display Custom Page Setup

A Page Setup window will appear:

Pic 73 Page Setup window

In the Header/Footer tab, you can insert the header and footer for each page in the printed paper. The header is a space on the top of the page, while footer is an area on the bottom of the page.

Pic 74 Header/Footer tab

3.6   Printing Worksheet

Printing in Excel is not as simple as in MS Word. You have to define the print area first. It's different with MS Word, where a page in MS Word will appear in a paper if printed directly.

Do steps below to print a worksheet in MS Excel:

1. Select areas (more than one cells) you want to print.

2. Click Page Layout tab. Click **Print Area > Set Print Area**.

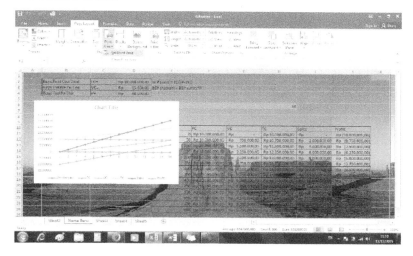

Pic 75 Click on Set Print Area button

3. Page Setup > Sheet window will appear. You can see the Print Area selected in text box **Print area**.

Pic 76 Print area window

4. Click **File > Print**.

Pic 77 Click on File > Print menu

5. You can see the print preview on the right side. You can also configure the printer properties (optional) in Print Properties.

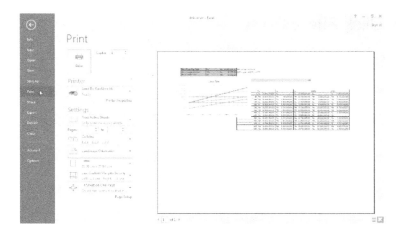

Pic 78 Print Preview

6. If everything is OK, then click Print icon to do the print work.

4. EXCEL FORMULAS

The core of spreadsheet software is formulas. This makes Excel is very intelligent and can be used to do many spreadsheet calculations. This is because Excel has the capability to create so many formulas, formula with built-in functions or formula you can define it by yourself.

Excel formulas can be directly used without having to install plug-ins or add-ins first. This is because this function is supported by default in Excel.

4.1   Create Formulas

All formulas in Excel, no matter how complex they are, mainly set up with a simple technique.

1. Click the cell you want to create the formula.

2. Click equal (=) symbol on your keyboard. All equal symbol will tell Excel that you will create a formula.

4.2 Cell Reference

You can create a formula that gets value from another cell. You just have to reference the other cell to the formula so that the formula can count the value based on the value. This method has many advantages:

1. If the value in other cell changed, the formula will be updated directly and display new value.

2. In certain case, using cell reference, you can copy the formula to another cell (usually adjacent cells) in a worksheet, and the reference in the newly copied will dynamically update to the cell.

The easiest method to reference cell is using a mouse, just click the cell you want to reference, this will automatically reference the cell into the formula (after the = sign).

4.3   Mathematics Formulas

Basic of mathematical formulas are the arithmetical operator, such as multiply, divide, add, and subtract. We'll demonstrate how to use the arithmetical operator in steps below:

1. There is two numerical value we want to operate using Excel math formula.

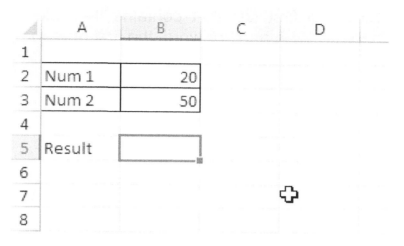

Pic 79 Two numerical values will be calculated

2. Enter equal sign to start formula creation.

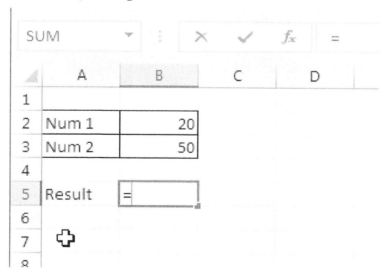

Pic 1.80 Inserting equal sign to start formula creation

3. Click the first cell that contains the value to operate, or in another word, the first operand.

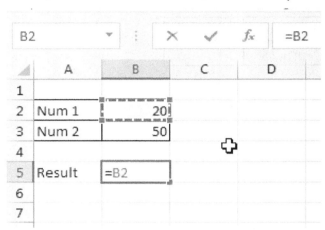

Pic 1.81 Click on the first cell

4. Insert the operator, for this example, I'll use plus operator to perform addition.

| SUM | ▼ | ⋮ | ✕ | ✓ | *fx* | =B2+ |

	A	B	C	D	
1					
2	Num 1	20			
3	Num 2	50			
4					
5	Result	=B2+			
6					
7					
8					

Pic 1.82 Inserting the additional operator

5. Choose the second value as the second operand.

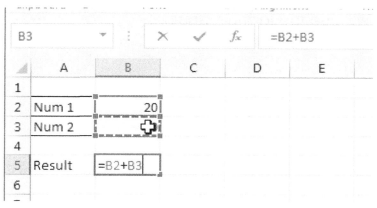

Pic 1.83 Select second value to operate, the second operand

6. Click Enter on your keyboard. This will make the formula inserted. You can see the formula written on the formula bar, and the result of the operation displayed in the cell.

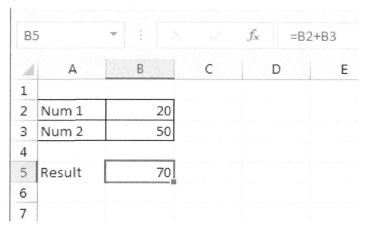

Pic 1.84 Formula already inserted

7. If you click your mouse on the cell again, you will see the formula again.

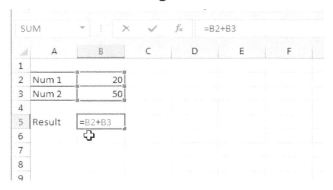

Pic 1.85 Excel formula appeared when you mouse click the cell

8. You can change the operator with * to do multiplication.

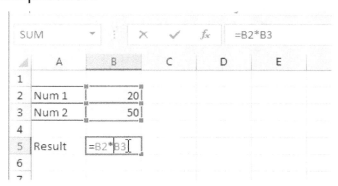

Pic 1.86 Changing the operator to perform multiplication

9. Click Enter, the result of the multiplication will be   displayed.

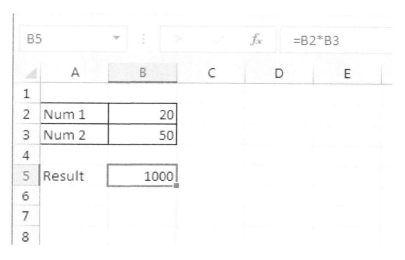

Pic 1.87 Result of the multiplication formula

10. To do division operation, change the operator to type division symbol (/).

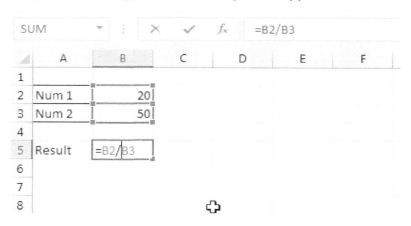

Pic 1.88 Changing the operator to /

11. The result of the formula will be updated in a aftermath of the division.

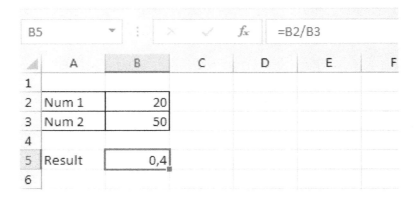

Pic 1.89 The result updated because of division formula

12. To change to subtraction operation, use minus (-) symbol as an operator.

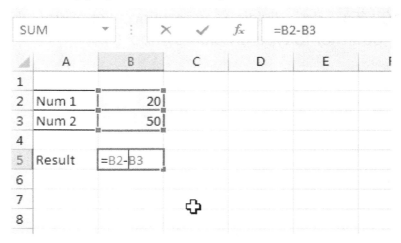

1.90 Minus (-) symbol as an operator for subtraction

13. The result will be updated

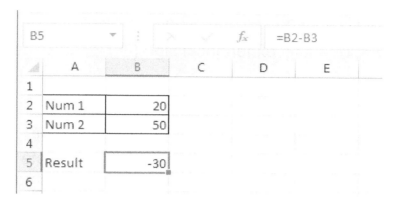

Pic 1.91 Subtraction result

14. From the above steps, you can see those arithmetic operators used in Excel formula are the same with regular mathematics.

Arithmetical operators in Excel have symbols:

1. Subtraction, minus sign (-).

2. Addition, plus sign(+)

3. Division, slash sign (/)

4. Multiplication, asterisk sign (*)

5. Exponential, exponential sign (^)

4.4 Named Ranges

The range is a collection more than one cell. To ease the formula creation, you can create a named range. This will make the function more readable. To create named ranges, you could use steps below:

1. For example, there is a table where the second column will be defined as a named range.

	A	B	C	D	E
1					
2		Product Sales Report			
3		Temperature	Sales		
4		15	140		
5		14	120		
6		13	140		
7		15	120		
8		14	140		
9		14	200		
10		51	120		
11		21	123		
12		23	130		
13		22	143		
14					
15					
16					
17					
18					

C15

2. Select the range you want to be identified, right click and click **Define Name** menu.

Pic 1.93 Range selected

3. **New Name** window appears, insert the name for this field in the **Name** text box.

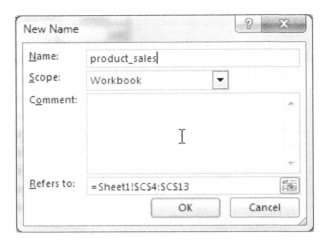

Pic 1.94 Inserting name for selected range

4. When you choose one cell that is a member of the range, the name still unidentified.

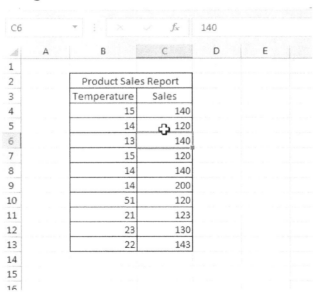

5. But if you choose all the cells of the range, the name will be seen in the top-left text box, adjacent to the formula box.

	A	B	C	D	E	F
1						
2		Product Sales Report				
3		Temperature	Sales			
4		15	140			
5		14	120			
6		13	140			
7		15	120			
8		14	140			
9		14	200			
10		51	120			
11		21	123			
12		23	130			
13		22	143			
14						
15						
16						

Pic 1.96 Name of the designated range seen on the top left text box

6. Using named range, creating formula easier. Because you can make the formula more readable, for example, you can just create AVERAGE (named_range) to calculate the mean value from all the cells in the range.

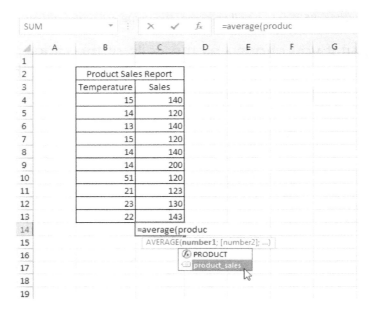

Pic 1.97 Named range used on formula

7. If the named_range's name selected (you put your pointer there), all cells within the named_range will be chosen.

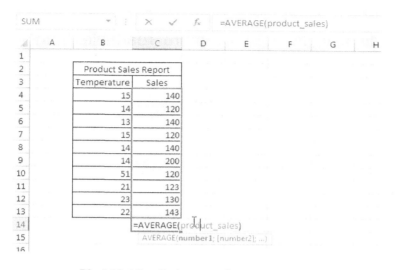

Pic 1.98 All cells in named range selected

8. If the formula created, the formula bar will display the formula more readable than just creating using cells address.

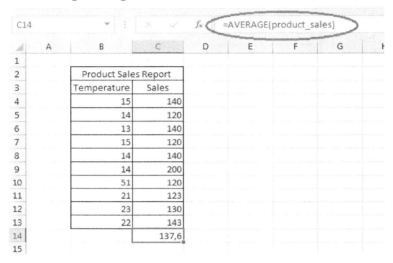

Pic 1.99 Named range

5. IF AND LOGIC FUNCTIONS

To make the formula more advanced, you can use If and other logic functions. This feature will create a logic test to manage the flow of the formula. The value compared using IF and other logic functions is called boolean. Boolean value only has two variations, True or False.

5.1 AND

AND will return TRUE only if the two operand has value TRUE. The syntax is:

```
= AND ( operand_1 , operand_2 , ... operand_255 )
```

You can see on steps below:

1. There are two values, TRUE and FALSE.

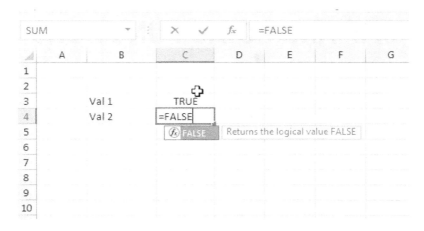

Pic 100 Two values TRUE and FALSE as an operand

2. Type an equal sign, and use function AND followed by (then enter the operand, and followed by).

Pic 101 Entering AND function and inserting the operand

3. The result is false because one of the operands is false.

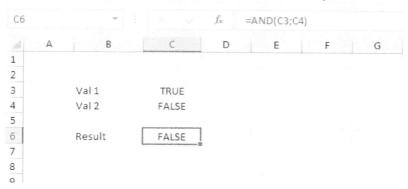

Pic 102 Result of the AND function is FALSE

5.2   OR

OR function will return a TRUE value if at least one of the operands has value TRUE. The syntax will be like this:

```
= OR ( operand_1 , operand_2 , ... operand_255 )
```

The creation process of this OR function:

1. Enter equal sign = and type "OR" to insert.

2. Choose the range of operands you want to operate using function OR.

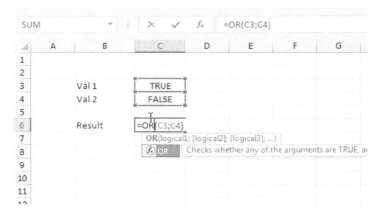

Pic 103 Select range of operands to be compared using OR

3. The result of the OR function is True because one of the operands has a True value.

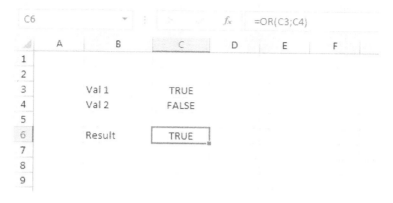

Pic 104 Result of OR function

5.3 IF

IF function is used for decision-making based on logical value. You can define what action is taken when the if-test valued True and other activities when the if-test valued FALSE.

1. Click on the cell to create a formula using IF function.

2. Enter equal sign to start creating the formula.

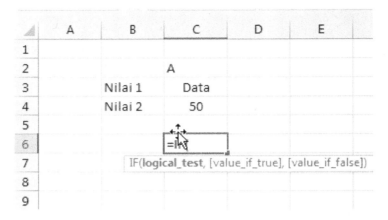

Pic 105 Creating Formula with IF function

3. Create the logical test, for example, we want to create whether cell C4's value bigger than 50.

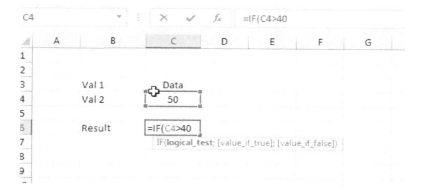

Pic 106 Logical test

4. Define text to display when the value True, and text to display if value False.

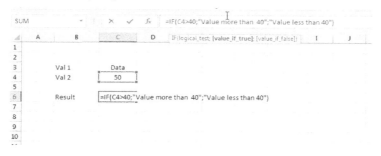

Pic 107 Defining text value to display if true and if false

5. Click Enter, because the if-test is True, then the text displayed will be the first text.

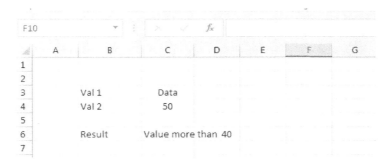

Pic 108 Second text is displayed because the if-test equal to FALSE

6. If the test value changed, so the if-test valued False, the first text will be displayed.

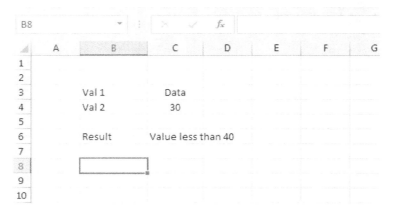

Pic 109 If C4's value updated, the if-test will be False

6. WORKING WITH DATA

When dealing with data, there are many techniques to make data editing easier. You will learn some of them here.

6.1   Freeze Panes

If the data very broad and cannot display in a single window, you could freeze some panel so that you can slide some data, while other data were frozen.

Here is the example:

1. There is a full data we want to freeze.

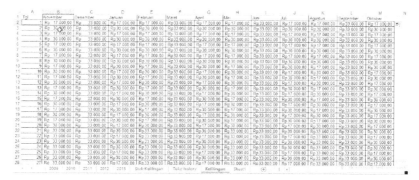

Pic 110 Wide data we want to freeze

2. Click the cell which we want to freeze. This feature is basically below the data column header, and row header, or the column or row that freeze (stay unscrolled).

	A	B	C	D
1	Tgl	November	Desember	Januari
2		1	Rp 17.000,00	Rp 33.000,00	Rp 17.000
3		2	Rp 30.000,00	Rp 33.000,00	Rp 30.000
4		3	Rp 17.000,00	Rp 33.000,00	Rp 17.000
5		4	Rp 30.000,00	Rp 33.000,00	Rp 30.000
6		5	Rp 17.000,00	Rp 33.000,00	Rp 17.000

Pic 111 Click on the cell that will act as

3. Click **View** tab on the ribbon, then click **Freeze Panes > Freeze Panes**.

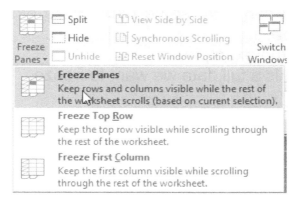

Pic 112 Freeze Panes menu to activate Freeze Panes

4. After the freeze, if you slide horizontally the data will be scrolled horizontally, but the left column stays unscrolled.

	A	L	M	N	O
1	Tgl	September	Oktober		
2	1	Rp 33.000,00	Rp 17.000,00		
3	2	Rp 33.000,00	Rp 30.000,00		
4	3	Rp 33.000,00	Rp 17.000,00		
5	4	Rp 33.000,00	Rp 30.000,00		
6	5	Rp 33.000,00	Rp 17.000,00		
7	6	Rp 33.000,00	Rp 30.000,00		
8	7	Rp 33.000,00	Rp 17.000,00		
9	8	Rp 33.000,00	Rp 30.000,00		
10	9	Rp 33.000,00	Rp 30.000,00		
11	10	Rp 33.000,00	Rp 17.000,00		
12	11	Rp 33.000,00	Rp 30.000,00		
13	12	Rp 33.000,00	Rp 17.000,00		
14	13	Rp 33.000,00	Rp 30.000,00		
15	14	Rp 33.000,00	Rp 17.000,00		
16	15	Rp 33.000,00	Rp 30.000,00		
17	16	Rp 33.000,00	Rp 17.000,00		
18	17	Rp 33.000,00	Rp 30.000,00		
19	18	Rp 33.000,00	Rp 17.000,00		
20	19	Rp 33.000,00	Rp 30.000,00		
21	20	Rp 33.000,00	Rp 17.000,00		
22	21	Rp 33.000,00	Rp 30.000,00		

Pic 113 Column B, C scrolled

5. If the data scrolled vertically, the rows below the header row would scroll above.

	A	L	M	N	O
1	Tgl	September	Oktober		
22	21	Rp 33.000,00	Rp 30.000,00		
23	22	Rp 33.000,00	Rp 17.000,00		
24	23	Rp 33.000,00	Rp 30.000,00		
25	24	Rp 33.000,00	Rp 30.000,00		
26	25	Rp 33.000,00	Rp 17.000,00		
27	26	Rp 33.000,00	Rp 30.000,00		
28	27	Rp 33.000,00	Rp 17.000,00		
29	28	Rp 33.000,00	Rp 30.000,00		
30	29	Rp 33.000,00	Rp 17.000,00		
31	30	Rp 33.000,00	Rp 30.000,00		
32	31	Rp 33.000,00	Rp 17.000,00		
33	Jml Total				
34					
35					
36					
37					

Pic 114 Rows scrolled while the header does not

6. To remove the Freeze Panes effect, click View tab, then click **Freeze panes > Unfreeze Panes**.

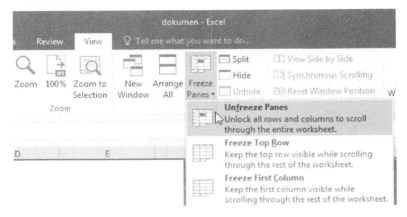

Pic 115 Click for Panes > Unfreeze Panes

7. After unfrozen, the data will fully back appear.

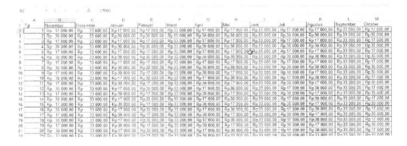

Pic 116 The data appear full after unfreeze

6.2   Sorting Data

A numeric and alphanumeric data can be sorted using certain criteria. Here is the example:

1. For example, there is a data of the worker.

Pic 117 Data of worker

2. For numerical value, you can sort from small to large by selecting the cells, then click **Sort > Sort Smallest to Largest**. This will sort the numeric data from smallest to largest

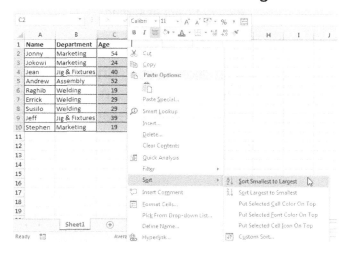

Pic 118 Sort Smallest to largest

3. The data on the column will be sorted automatically, while the data in another column will be adjusted too because I select **Expand the selection**.

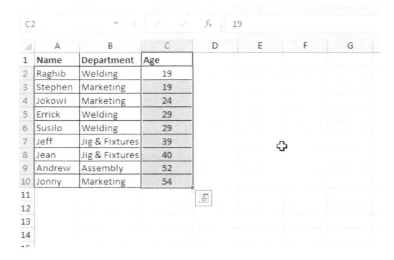

	A	B	C	D	E	F	G
1	Name	Department	Age				
2	Raghib	Welding	19				
3	Stephen	Marketing	19				
4	Jokowi	Marketing	24				
5	Errick	Welding	29				
6	Susilo	Welding	29				
7	Jeff	Jig & Fixtures	39				
8	Jean	Jig & Fixtures	40				
9	Andrew	Assembly	52				
10	Jonny	Marketing	54				
11							
12							
13							
14							

Pic 119 Result of sorting

6.4   Filtering Data

Filtering data will make Excel only display data that match the criteria. Here is an example:

1. Click on the column to be filtered.

2. Right-click and choose **Filter > Filter by selected cell's value**.

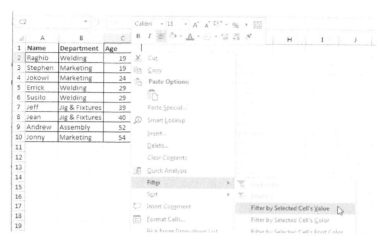

Pic 120 Filtering by selected cell's value

3. All of the table content will be empty. This is happening because everything is filtered.

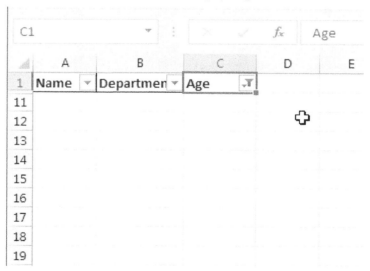

Pic 121 Table content empty because everything is filtered

4. Click on filter icon, then choose Select All to display all data.

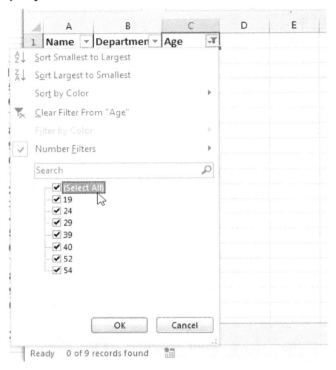

Pic 122 Select all to display everything

5. All the content of the table will be displayed.

6. You can also filter some data to be displayed by checking the value you want to show.

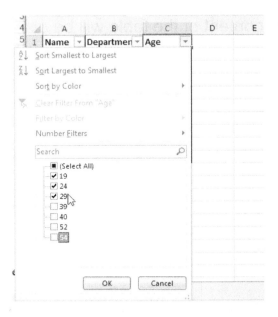

Pic 124 Checking on a particular value to display

7. The data selected will be displayed.

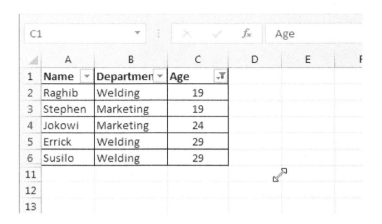

Pic 125 Data selected will be displayed

8. You can also create criteria for filtering. For example to display data which has more than a value, right-click on the column, then **Number Filters > Greater Than**.

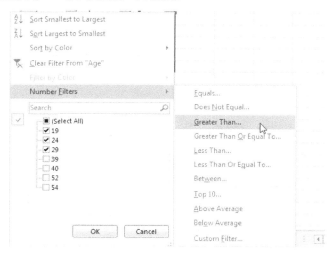

Pic 126 Number Filters > Greater than

9. Enter the value for filtering, for example, 50 on **Is bigger than** a text box. This value will only display values greater than 50.

Pic 127 Entering criteria for filtering

10. Data that will be displayed will be the data with value > 50.

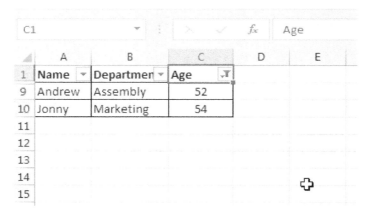

Pic 128 Data presented will have data value > 50

11. To remove filtering, click **Sort & Filter > Filter**. The filtering will be deleted.

Pic 129 Menu to remove filtering

6.5 Table

A regular data in Excel can be formatted as Excel table. This feature will make creating chart and table's data manipulation easier. Here is how you can create regular data as a table:

1. Choose all the cells you want to incorporate into a table.

Pic 130 Selecting Range to be incorporated into an Excel table

2. Click Format as Table and choose the table style format you want.

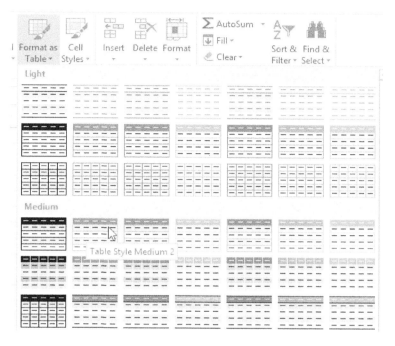

Pic 131 Select table style format

3. The range will be chosen, you can see dotted line encircling your table. If the table has a header, check **My table has headers**.

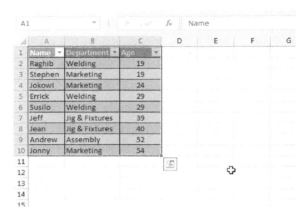

Pic 132 Click OK to create a table from the selected range

4. Click OK, the range you selected will become an Excel table. When the data became a table, a filtering arrow will appear on the header.

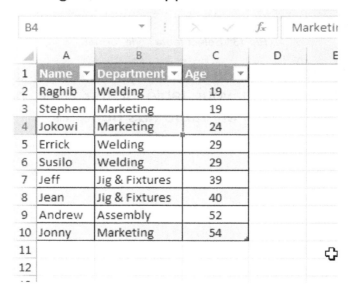

Pic 133 Filtering arrow on each column's header

5. When you select a cell outside, the range still formatted as a table. A table can also be selected by inserting the table's name on **Name** text box.

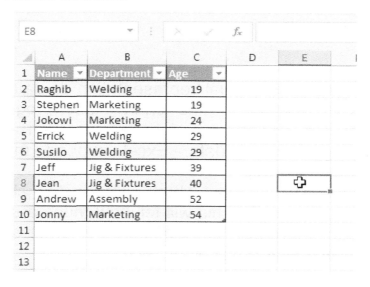

Pic 134 Ranges already formatted as a table

7. CHART & PIVOT TABLE

The chart is a visual representation of data in Excel's worksheet. The chart makes regular user can understand data easier than just reading numeric data. Excel support many charts as follows:

Chapter 1   Pie chart: Used to show percentage. This will tell how much a slice of the data value compared to other slice and overall values of the cell.

Chapter 2   Column chart: Used to compare items. Each column shows a value of data.

Chapter 3   Bar chart: similar with column chart, just located horizontally and not vertically like a column.

Chapter 4   Line chart: Nice to show the trend of data, from time to time.

Chart sometimes called as graphic. Besides the charts above, there are lots of another chart type in Excel.

7.1   Creating Chart

To create a graph, you should do three things:
First inserting data, no matter what type of chart you want to create, you should enter data to the worksheet.

When entering data into a worksheet, please consider some pieces of information below:

1. Don't let empty cell or row/column between data. If there is an empty row or column between data, this will make Excel Chart Wizard not efficient. Hence will make creating chart harder, you have to select data manually.

2. If you can, insert data in column style. You just need to type the data name in the header, and then the data series for that header below the header name in one column.

Second is choosing data.

	A	B	C	D
1	Average Precipitation for World Cities (mm)			
2				
3	Location	January	April	July
4	Acapulco	10	5	208
5	Amsterdam	69	53	76
6	Anchorage	17	13	42.5
7	Dallas	48	87.5	62
8	Glasgow	110	50	61
9	Madrid	39	48	11
10	New York	99	100	115
11	Tokyo	101	121	189
12	Toronto	55.2	65.4	71
13				

Drag with mouse

Pic 135 Choosing data

To pick data, you have to:

1. Click from the top-left of the data

2. Drag pointer across data, so every cell should be selected.

The third step is by choosing what methods were taken, using the chart wizard or manual.

7.2   Creating Column Chart

To show how to create a chart, I will demonstrate how to build a column chart. By following this example, you can create another type of charts easily, because basically, all chart is the same.

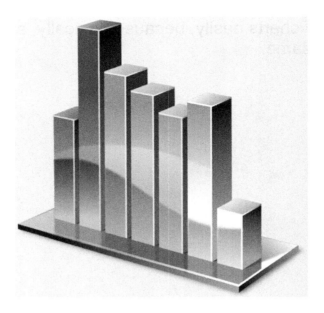

Pic 136 Column chart

Look at the example below:
1. The data for this example like this:

Salesman	Total Sales
Jimmi	10000
Joan	12000
Tri	18000
Tony	11000
Jerry	9000

2. Select all the table, including the text in the header.

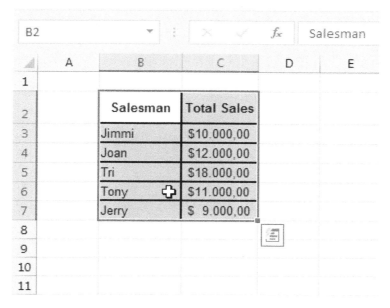

Pic 137 Selecting all table component

3. Click Insert Chart, because the chart we want to create is a column chart, choose Column.

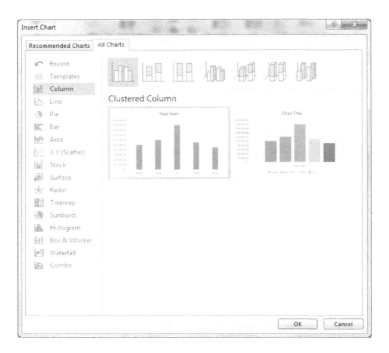

Pic 138 Creating Column

4. Click on one sub-type of the column type.

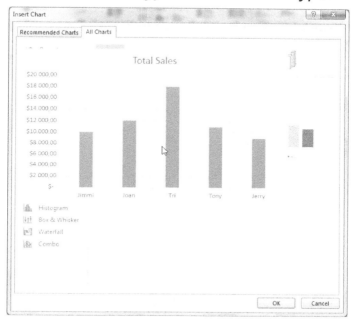

Pic 139 Choosing sub-type from the Column chart

5. A table will be created automatically.

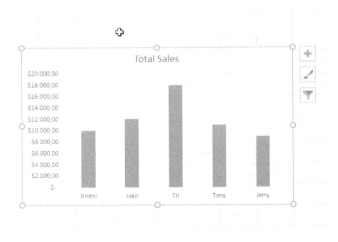

Pic 140 Column table created automatically

6. You can also create a table by clicking Insert > Column then choose sub-type of the column table you want to create.

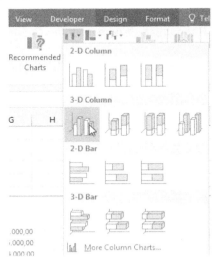

Pic 141 Choosing column table type

7. A new table will be created.

Pic 142 New table created

8. The table already created can be customized, for example, the horizontal lines can be deleted by click on one of the lines, then right-click and click **Delete**.

Pic 143 Using Delete menu to delete horizontal lines

9. The horizontal line will be deleted from the table.

Pic 144 Horizontal line deleted from the table

10. To format certain columns on the chart, right click and choose **Format Data Point**.

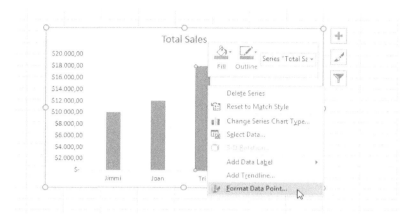

Pic 145 Menu Format Data Point to format columns on the chart

11. The first tab is Series options. You can change the depth and width properties of the series options. Select by changing the depth and width.

Pic 146 Series options

113

12. Fill tab is used to manage colors, pattern, or picture to fill the columns.

Pic 147 Format Data Point

13. After the column is changed, the column will have a different style.

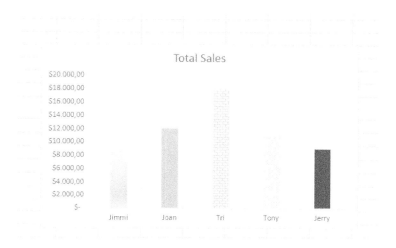

Pic 148 Column have different styles

14. In Border color, you can define what type of border for the columns.

Pic 149 Border Color

15. The columns will be bordered.

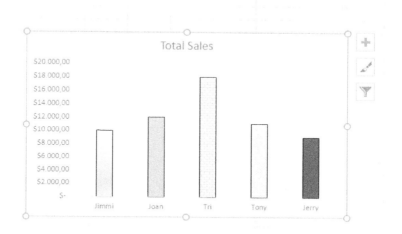

Pic 150 Columns after bordered

16. In Shadow, you can give shadows for the data points/columns.

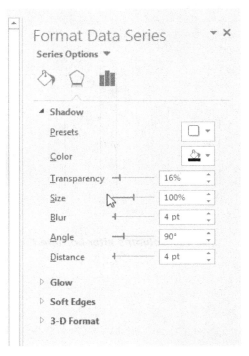

Pic 151 Configuring Shadow

17. In a 3D Format, you can configure the 3D style for data points/columns.

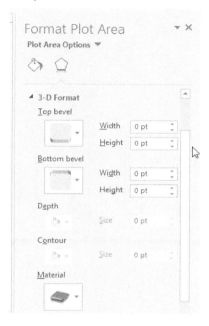

Pic 152 Configuring 3D-format for data points

18. The format of the columns or data points from the chart will be different from the default condition.

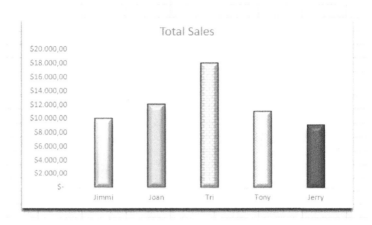

Pic 153 Data points of the chart after formatted

19. To change the title of the chart, you can click the title box.

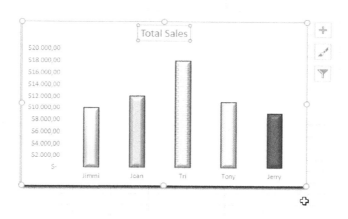

Pic 154 Clicking the title box to change chart's title

20. Type the new text for the title.

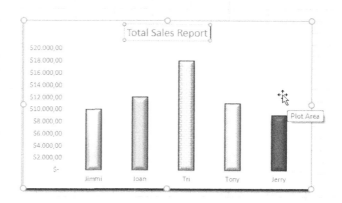

Pic 155 Typing new text for the title

21. To see data source, right-click and choose **Select data**.

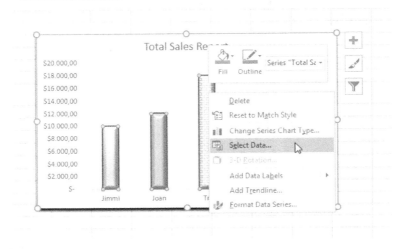

Pic 156 Menu to Select Data

22. You can see a series of data used as legend entries and axis labels.

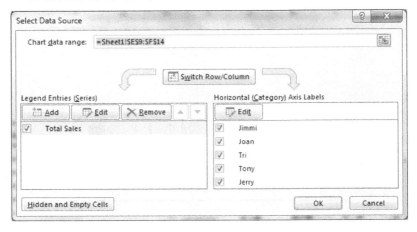

Pic 157 Data source

23. When the Data Source window opened, you can see which column act as legend entries and Axis labels.

	Salesman	Total Sales
5		
6		
7		
8		
9	Salesman	Total Sales
10	Jimmi	$10.000,00
11	Joan	$12.000,00
12	Tri	$18.000,00
13	Tony	$11.000,00
14	Jerry	$ 9.000,00
15		
16		
17		

Pic 158 Data source

24. You can change the type of chart to a different kind of column by clicking **Column > Other Column Type**.

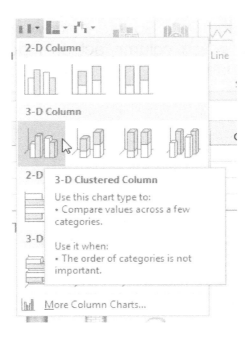

Pic 159 Column > Other Column Type

7.3   Pivot Table

A table can be pivoted to create a pivot table. This table will help you to see information more clearly. You can see some aggregated data which it cannot be seen using the standard table. Here is how to create a pivot table:
1. Click on **Insert > Pivot table**.

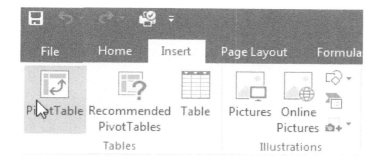

Pic 160 Click Insert > PivotTable

2. Choose the range that has data to make the table and click **OK**.

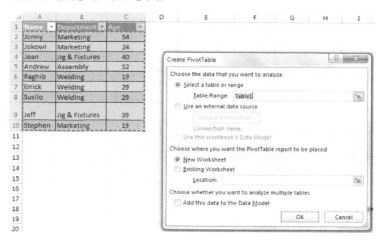

Pic 161 Choosing range to create a pivot table

3. Pivot table box appeared, but you haven't seen any columns entered.

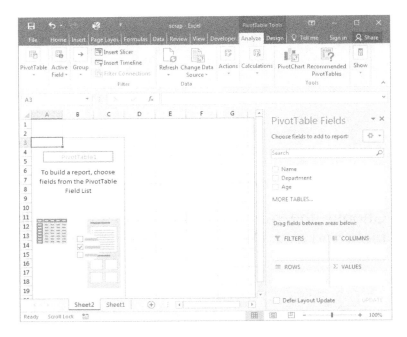

Pic 162 Pivot table entered

4. For example, if we want to know the average age for each department, you can enter pic below:

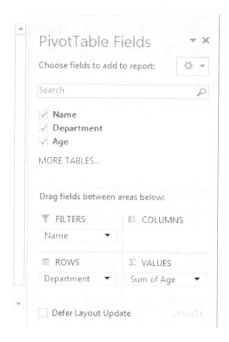

Pic 163 Inserting column by dragging to the right side

5. You can see the SUM of age.

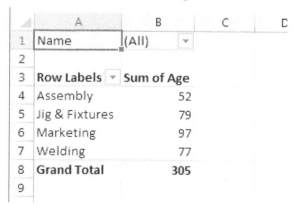

	A	B	C	D
1	Name	(All)		
2				
3	Row Labels	Sum of Age		
4	Assembly	52		
5	Jig & Fixtures	79		
6	Marketing	97		
7	Welding	77		
8	**Grand Total**	305		
9				

Pic 164 Pivot table for the sum for Age

6. To change the aggregation type, click on Sum of Age and click **Value Field Settings**.

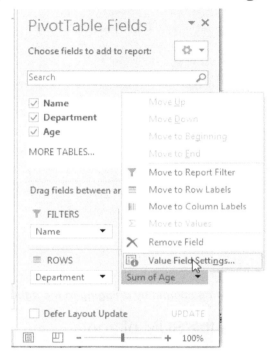

Pic 165 Choosing Value Field Settings

7. Choose **Summarize type** to **Average**.

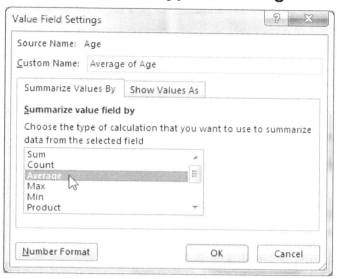

Pic 167 Choosing Summarize Type to Average

8. You can see the average age of each department.

Pic 168 Average age per department

ABOUT THE AUTHOR

Ali Akbar is a Visual Basic.NET Author who has more than 10 years of experience in the architecture and has been using Visual Basic.NET for more than 15 years. He has worked on design pro-jects ranging from department store to transportation systems to the Semarang project. He is the all–time best-selling Visual Basic.NET author and was cited as favorite programming author. Zico P. Putra is a senior engineering technician, CAD consultant, author, & trainer with 10 years of experience in several design fields. He continues his PhD in Queen Mary University of London. Ali Akbar is an AutoCAD Author who has more than 10 years of experience in the architecture and has been using AutoCAD for more than 15 years. He has worked on design projects ranging from department store to transportation systems to the Semarang project. He is the all–time bestselling AutoCAD author and was cited as favorite CAD author. Find out more at https://www.amazon.com/Zico-Pratama-Putra/e/B06XDRTM1G/

CAN I ASK A FAVOUR?

If you enjoyed this book, found it useful or otherwise then I would really appreciate it if you would post a short review on Amazon. I do read all the reviews personally so that I can continually write what people are wanting.
If you would like to leave a review, then please visit the link below:
https://www.amazon.com/dp/B06XS99PKP
Thanks for your support!

Made in United States
North Haven, CT
30 December 2023

46824818R10078